Wiggly Workers

Written by Diane Cheek
Illustrated by Diane Daly

AuthorHouse™
1663 Liberty Drive
Bloomington, IN 47403
www.authorhouse.com
Phone: 1-800-839-8640

© 2011 Diane Cheek. All rights reserved.

No part of this book may be reproduced, stored in a retrieval system,
or transmitted by any means without the written permission of the author.

First published by AuthorHouse   7/27/2011

ISBN: 978-1-4634-0022-4 (sc)

Library of Congress Control Number: 2011907545

Printed in the United States of America

Certain stock imagery © Thinkstock.

**To worm lovers
and**

To the memory of Mary Appelhof

scientist, educator, and worm enthusiast

Worms live in darkness. They don't like the light.
That is the reason they keep out of sight.

Deep in the earth or inside a bin, that's where you'll find them as their story begins.

Worms slither and slide and make not a sound; but no better workers can ever be found.

Deep in the dirt, away from the light, worms are at work all day and all night.

Without eyes to guide them, they still find their way, to tunnel the earth while we work and we play.

Why is this important you might want to say?
Worms are earth helpers; they encourage decay.

They eat rotting matter; it's gross I must say! Yet to them it's delicious; they love it that way!

Squirmy and moist they tunnel along

leaving the soil air filtered and strong.

If you have a worm bin you know this is true. Our red wiggler friends make magic for you!

Inside the bin eating left over stuff, worms munch on green garbage for breakfast and lunch. What happens next is something to know; our red wiggler friends have something to show.

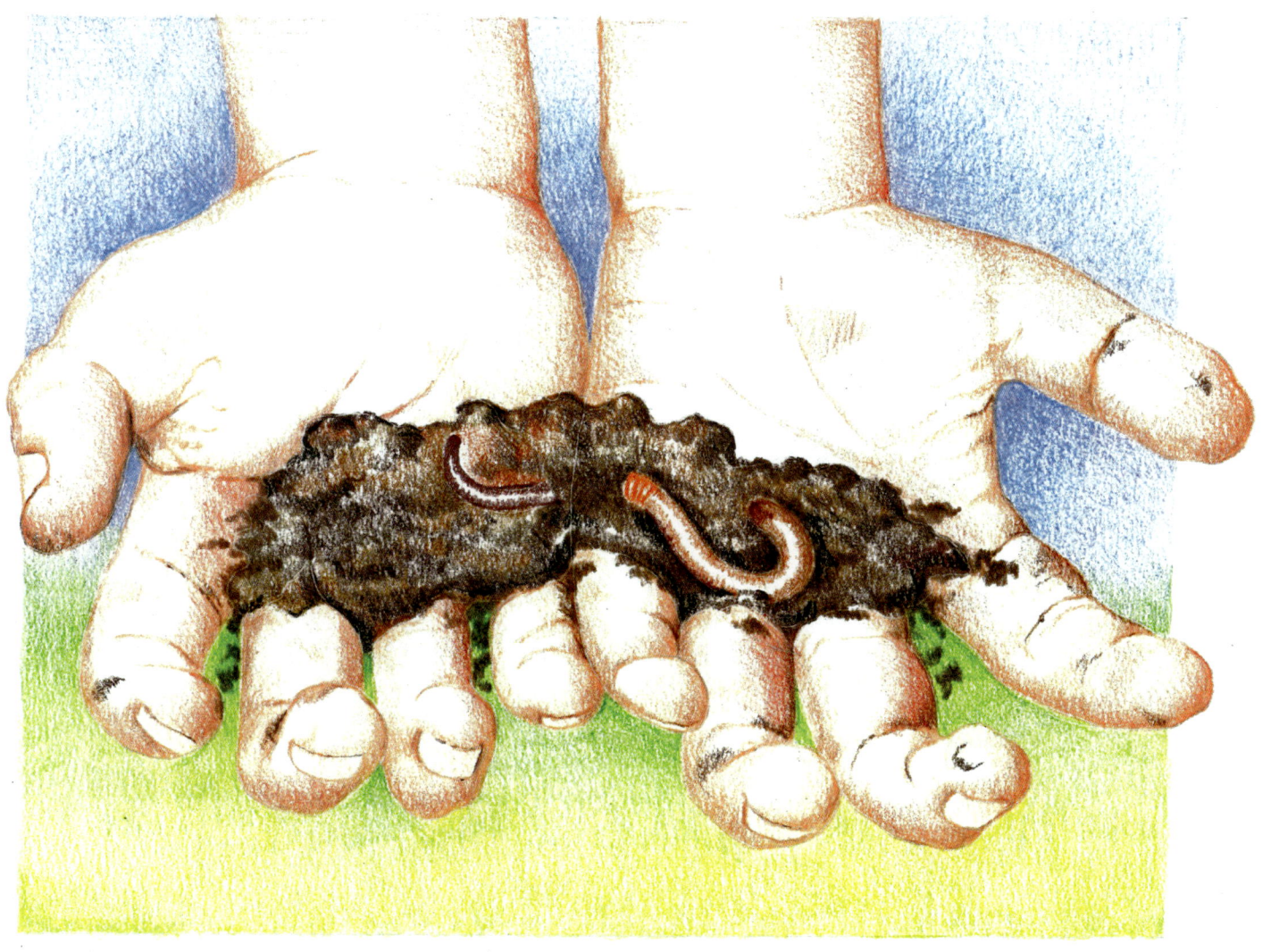

Out of their bodies come nutrients grand, *compost* for us to give back to the land.

Call it <u>*Black Gold*</u>, <u>*Compost*</u> or <u>*Castings*</u> all of them make plants happy and lasting!

Plants love compost; for them it's a treat!

Their roots become strong so flowers can shine. It's just what they need, everyday, all the time!

Hurrah for the worms! Good friends to the earth! Come give a smile and giggle with mirth!

Now that you know, please keep this in mind. The smallest of things are simply divine!

The End ...or is it?
This might be a beginning!

Can you find some worms?
Do you have a worm bin?

Worm Bin Basics

(*Red Wiggler Worms* are used in worm bins.
To obtain Red Wigglers see suggestions below.)

1. **Make The Bin:** A dark plastic 18 gal. storage bin is fine for a worm bin.

2. **Give Them Air:** Using a drill and 3/8 drill bit, make several holes on all sides of the bin.

3. **Make Their Bed:** Shred about 8 pounds of black and white newspaper. Dampen the shredded newspaper with a spray bottle until it's moist but not soggy. When the bin is about 2/3 full of damp shredded newsprint, mix in 1 or 2 cups of garden soil.

4. **Move Them In:** Put 1 or 2 pounds of Red Wigglers into the bin and watch them go down into the bin! (Remember… they don't like the light!)

5. **Feed Them:** Every week collect about 4 to 5 cups (3 pounds) of chopped vegetables, fruit, coffee grounds, tea bags. Put the food under the damp, shredded paper. If needed, use a spray bottle to keep the bin contents moist.

6. **Where They Live:** A shady spot in the yard or garden works well in mild climates. In very cold or very hot temperatures the container needs to be inside. A good temperature range for Red Wigglers is 50 to 80 degrees.

7. **And Then…** In about 9 to 10 months the contents in the bin will have changed from newspaper and food scraps, to compost made from worms!

Bait stores and some plant nurseries sell Red Wiggler Worms. Many websites have good information, plus they sell worm bins and Red Wiggler Worms.

Good resources are: www.wormwoman.com
The author's e-mail: scwormlady@gmail.com

Words to Know

Tiger Worms, Red Wigglers ... the common names used for the type of worms that like to live in a contained space such as a worm bin

Eisenia fetida ... the scientific name for Tiger Worms and Red Wigglers

Castings ... worm poop, rich in nutrients for plants

Worm Compost (Vermicompost) ... food that has moved through a worm's system (worm poop) plus other decomposed organic material resulting in nutrient-rich, dirt-like material

Decay ... the rotting process of organic material by living decomposers (bacteria)

Nutrients ... elements that are absorbed for healthy plant growth

Mouth-flap ...a tiny flap (unseen by human eyes), located above the mouth; this flap scoops food into the worm's mouth

Saddle (Clitellum) ...the thick band on mature worms, where cocoon material is secreted

Segments ... ringed parts of the worm's body

Bristles (setae) ... tiny stiff hairs on the worm's body (unseen by human eyes), that help the worm move

Anus ... the small opening at the tail end of the worm where castings are expelled

Worms Inside and Out

Worms are invertebrates ... they have no backbone, they have no bones at all!

No eyes   No feet
No nose   No hands
No ears   No lungs
No bones

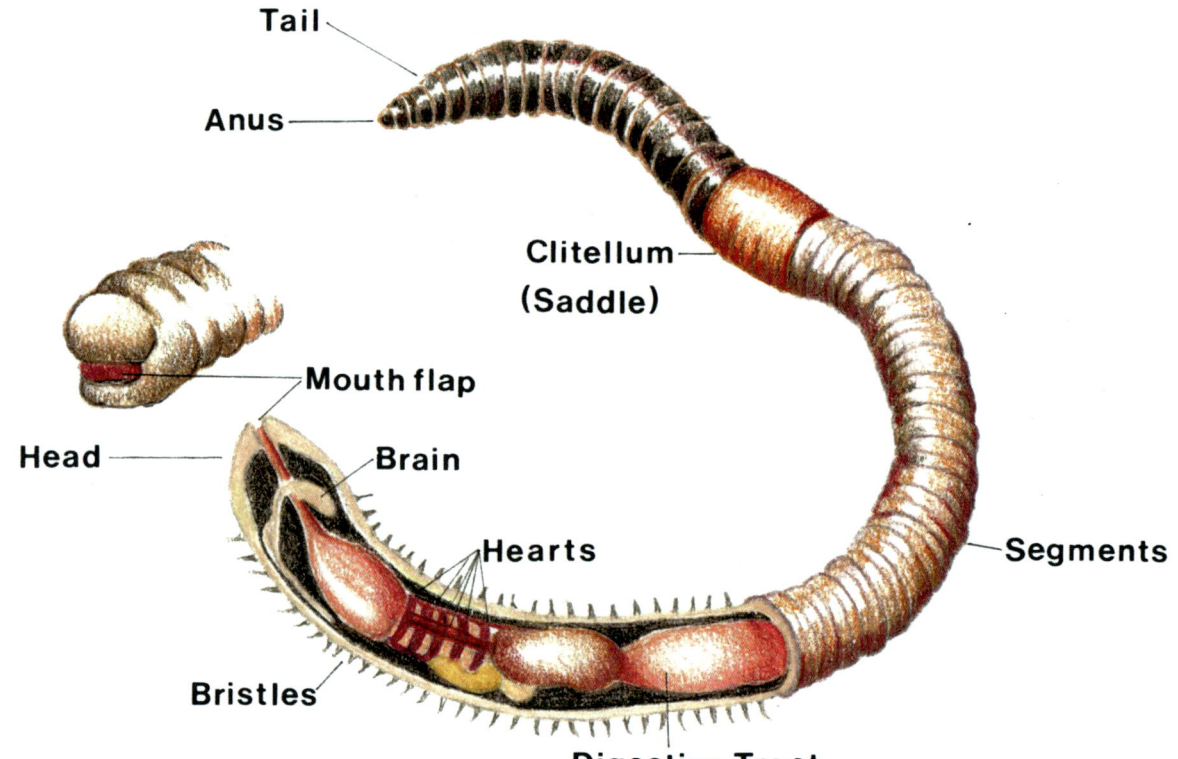

About the author and illustrator

Diane Cheek is a retired primary school teacher. This is her first book. She lives in Southern California with her husband, two cats, a desert tortoise, and hundreds of Red Wiggler Worms.

Diane Daily has returned to her love of illustration after a career in graphic design. She is a member of the Botanical Artists Guild of Southern California and resides in Irvine California with her husband and two children.

Fun Facts About Worms

Red Wigglers reach maturity in 10 weeks.

There are more than 1,800 different kinds of worms.

Worms eat almost half their body weight everyday!

A worm's body is made up of about 250 segments.

Worms breathe through their skin.

The life span of most worms is less than a year, but in a bin, Red Wigglers can live up to four years!

Baby worms come from tiny worm eggs also called cocoons.

Made in United States
North Haven, CT
23 March 2023

34452079R00018